# Granddad Bud

## A Veterans Day Story

Sharon Ferry

*AuthorHouse™*
*1663 Liberty Drive*
*Bloomington, IN 47403*
*www.authorhouse.com*
*Phone: 1-800-839-8640*

*First published by AuthorHouse    8/9/2010*

*ISBN: 978-1-4520-5029-4 (sc)*

*Library of Congress Control Number: 2010909861*

*Printed in the United States of America*
*Bloomington, Indiana*

*This book is printed on acid-free paper.*

authorHOUSE®

For my grandparents, John "Bud" and Alice Hendrick

Special thanks to the
Pennsylvania Veterans Museum, Media, PA

Today is Veterans Day. I'm not exactly sure what that means, but I do know it's something to do with all the people who fought in wars for our country. They're called veterans.

My Granddad Bud is a veteran. He was in the Navy in World War II. That was a long time ago. I know because he was a young man back then, and now he's 90 years old.

Granddad Bud is coming to my school today. For Veterans Day, our school has invited some veterans to come in. We're having an assembly that was organized by some of the teachers and parents. There are going to be some speakers, including Granddad. Our school band is playing and we're having refreshments afterward.

I don't really know what Granddad Bud is going to say. I sometimes hear him tell stories about the war when we're at family parties. It doesn't seem that interesting to me – just like Veterans Day doesn't seem like a real interesting holiday (not like Halloween or the 4th of July).

My class is ready for the assembly.  We sit on the floor as the principal talks and introduces all the adults who are here today.  Granddad Bud walks in and waves to me.

Wow.  He looks really important wearing his jacket with all the medals and ribbons on it.  All the kids stop talking and look at him as he steps up to the microphone (even Jacob, who hardly ever stops talking).

Granddad Bud clears his throat and looks out at the audience. He tells us that Veterans Day was started in the year 1919, and was originally called Armistice Day. It was meant to celebrate the peace after the First World War. Years later, it was changed to Veterans Day as a way of honoring all veterans from all the wars that had taken place.

He tells us ways that people sometimes celebrate the day – by going to parades, visiting veterans in hospitals or making cards and collecting things to send to veterans groups. The President of the United States lays a wreath on the Tomb of the Unknown Soldier, which is a grave near Washington, DC that honors all veterans who never made it home.

Then Granddad Bud talks about being in the war. While he was in the Navy, he lived on a ship for over 2 years. He worked in the control room down below the deck. He and his friends worried about their ship being attacked – and sometimes it was – by enemy submarines or enemy planes. Granddad Bud tells us that Japan was the enemy back then. There were other countries that were fighting each other too during World War II.

Granddad Bud missed his family when he was away fighting in the war. He would get letters, but sometimes it was hard for the mail to be delivered to his ship and he wouldn't hear from his wife and daughter for a long time. Sometimes they didn't get a letter from him for a long time either. Then they would worry that something bad had happened to him.

Nothing bad did happen to Granddad Bud, but some of his friends died in the war. He says it still makes him sad to think about all the brave men and women who lost their lives fighting for their country. He says that we should pray for them, and for all the people who are still serving in the military to help America to continue to be a free and great country.

**VIETNAM**

I look around me. Everyone is still quiet and they're all looking at my Granddad Bud. They seem to be amazed at his story of being in the war. When he's finished, some of the other veterans have a turn to talk. One of them was in the Vietnam War in the 1970's. One of the women served in the Gulf War in the 1990's. I can tell that all the kids think these veterans are really brave.

After the assembly, I get to talk to Granddad Bud. He winks at me as I walk over to him with some of the kids in my class. Lots of kids are gathered around him, asking questions about the war. He's very patient and answers each one. I feel so proud of him.

One of the students asks Granddad about the Veterans Museum, which is not too far from here. He tells us that we can visit any time we want and that schools can even go on field trips there to learn more about veterans and the wars in which they fought. He says that the slogan of the museum is, "Learn, Honor, Remember."

Learn, honor and remember . . .
I think that's what Granddad Bud helped us all do today.